MODERN-DAY SANDCASTLES

The Fall of Denominationalism

Virginia Mayer

ISBN 979-8-89130-998-2 (paperback)
ISBN 979-8-89130-999-9 (digital)

Christian Faith Publishing
832 Park Avenue
Meadville, PA 16335
www.christianfaithpublishing.com

Printed in the United States of America

What a dreamy day—the sun skipping in between fluffy puffs of marshmallow white clouds and crystal blue skies. The little family settled their beach blankets and umbrella not far from the frothing shoreline—and on the gleaming white sands of the Gulf Coast! They wanted to soak in every bit of this beach experience and pack it away in their memories of good things. It was going to be just the best family trip.

Among unloading and setting up a picnic lunch, Mom had her ever-watching eyes on her two curly headed munchkins running and dancing on the beach. For just a brief amount of time, though she watched the two in hot competition, they were building their own designed and engineered sandcastles. Dad was their consultant; Mom was the monitor to make sure one of those little angels didn't accidentally remove an entire suite of rooms from the other's dream castle.

"Lunch is ready! Come on! Let's wash our hands! Our food is almost ready!"

Mom had already begun slathering peanut butter and jelly onto the bread when out of the sound of the rolling surf came a scream followed by a torrent of tears!

"Look, Daddy! Look! Those waves washed away my beautiful castle! I had it just the way I wanted it, Daddy, and now it's all gone! I had it all worked out my way!" Every bit of this blonde mop of hair and curls along with her sand-covered body collapsed into her father's arms.

For just a bit, Dad rocked his bundle of love, aggravation, and frustration and quietly whispered to his little one, "Maybe God had a better plan in mind."

Several years ago, the Lord told me to write a book, and He gave me the title, *Modern-Day Sandcastles: The Fall of Denominationalism.* To be honest, this title evoked a bit of fear in my heart and spirit, *What are the people that I love and care for that belong to a denominational church going to think?* God has assured me of one thing: those that I love and those that love me will continue to love, considering our first love is Jesus Christ and not the denominations we all represent. Over the years, I have come into an uncompromising belief that obedience to God is far more important than sacrifice; having said that, obedience stirs my heart to seek God's will for my life even if it means writing a book about the body of believers that are preparing to be the bride of Christ that entails unity and not division among members. More and more believers have begun to see that nothing in God's holy Word details any description of denominations in heaven. Many of these same believers are questioning the purpose of denominationalism. Consequentially, judgment of this writing will come from the heart of the writing, not so much the style of how the message is presented, but more so what the message speaks to the hearts of the genuine believer.

This thought has been very strongly knocking in my spirit; we can no longer be afraid to be obedient to what God is calling us to do. I see and I hear things that are wrong being called right and things that are right being called wrong. Sound familiar? Absolutely! God tells us that in the end days right would be wrong and wrong would be right. I really didn't want to see all this turmoil in my lifetime; I didn't want to take a step toward telling people the denominational concept to which they gave their lives, their allegiance had caused a great deal of divisiveness that the church, the body of Christ, will and must overcome. However, God is calling all of His children to take their place within the body of Christ, the bride of Christ, to have a voice and speak truth so that those that are lost will know Jesus Christ as their Savior in unity. Who knows what God has been or is asking all of you to do in this season? If He is calling you, I surely hope you answer a lot quicker than I did! We are all on a journey called life. We are all trying to find our way to God's Will for our lives…sort of like treasure hunters. God describes this process in Proverbs 23:2, "It is the glory of God to conceal a matter; to search out a matter is the glory of kings." Does this mean we are kings looking for our way? Yes! Revelations 1:5–6 tells us, "And from Jesus Christ, Who is the faithful Witness…and hath us made kings and priests unto God." So God has made us kings and priests for glory! How amazing is that? Can't say I felt like a king, definitely not a priest, as I made the decision to be obedient and start this writing, but I was totally convinced my obedience was somehow going to give God the glory.

Which brings me to a thought about genuine believers, which is the key to this entire writing: the genuineness of our hearts to believe all that Scripture says. All my adult Christian life, I have heard this statement: "You cannot pick and choose what you want to believe in Holy Scripture." I agree with this statement, strongly! Remember Thomas, the disciple that was not in the room when Jesus made His appearance to them? They were so excited, especially when

He showed them His hands, His side! Can anyone of us imagine that very moment! These devoted men did not have to see these wounds, but they got that honor. It's hard to hold in the joy even writing these words down! Seeing and being with your risen Savior but also seeing those precious wounds that brought about our blood–bought freedom and paved the way to our eternity with God; the words are hard to come by to give justice to what these men might have been feeling…at least almost all of them. Let's not forget our friend Thomas.

> On the evening of that first day of the week, when the disciples were together, with the doors locked in fear of the Jews, Jesus came and stood among them and said, "Peace be with you!" After he said this, he showed them His Hands and side. The disciples were overjoyed when they saw the Lord. (John 20:19–20)

The disciples received a very special gift that day when Jesus "breathed on them and said, 'Receive the Holy Spirit.'" How exciting could this have been? Without a doubt, the disciples that were there were eager to share what had happened. But Thomas was a bit late to the game, but not too late. When Thomas came back to the disciples, they spoke passionately to Thomas about seeing the Lord. Thomas, being Thomas, told the disciples that he wouldn't believe until he saw with his own eyes. A week later, that happened! The disciples had gathered once again with locked doors, and this time, Thomas was there, and Jesus showed Thomas where to put his hands. Thomas then declared, "My Lord and my

God" (John 20:28). Now, this is great that Thomas saw and believed, but what Jesus told him after that stuck in my heart as a standard by which to measure the genuineness of my heart. Jesus told Thomas, "Because you have seen me, you have believed; blessed are those who have not seen and yet believed" (John 20:29). I want to be counted in that number of folks that believe without seeing Jesus in the natural. After all, look what happens when one believes with a simple pure faith: "Blessed are those who have not seen and yet believed."

A genuine believer believes not armed with just the knowledge that someone has passed down but with a heart that receives Jesus as his or her Savior in faith. Now, having offered a brief picture of differing types of believers, my thought is, *Does everyone believe in our God, the one and only God?* Is this one of the areas in which divisiveness separates us all into the multitudes of denominations and keeps us apart from each other? Aren't we all to believe in the unity of the body of Christ? God told us that He would one day bring us all to the bride's supper. Look at Ephesians 5:27 and Revelations 21.

More thoughts, questions flooded in, *Lord, I am not a writer. How am I to pen a book about the fall of denominationalism?* Or more to the point, *Lord, do You know how people are going to look at me after this book? Why do You want this book now?* I wanted to know these things before I jumped into writing about something an infinitesimal number of scholars know way more than I ever will. You know that moment when you either do or you don't? In the case of God's instruction, I did not want to ever be in that position of having to decide if I would trust Him to just do what He told me to do without a thought or just ignore Him. Truly, I want to tell you that I just accepted His instruction and jumped right into the task of writing, but I can't tell you that because it is not true. Refer to my opening sentence: "Several years ago." I must admit there have been times when I asked God, "Is it time, Lord, to write this book?" His response was quietness which I took to mean, "No, not yet." I think He was waiting for me to say, "Yes, Lord, I will get right on it!" Instead, I put off addressing His command; I put off starting this book. Not the proudest moment of my life.

Which brings me to today. I have felt that today, April 4, 2021, is the day to begin. So the book has begun. Truthfully, this book began in Genesis. No, this is not a comparison to the holy Word, the Bible; this book is not a copy of Martin Luther's 95 Theses nailed to the church in Guttenberg. My belief is that this book reflects God's heart of love for His children. Specifically, God said to write a book about the demise, the fall of denominations. I believe He wants everyone to know how very desperately His heart desires to have all His children together in His church. A little reminder here: God did not tell me to spread the word to go out and shut down all the denominations on the planet. What and how this message is received and utilized was not a part of His instructions to me. Not being a theologian or a Bible scholar, all I have to offer is obedience to His request to write a book about the crumbling of denominationalism with all the passion in my heart to be obedient and with the limited knowledge I possess about denominationalism. I believe He wanted this to be a reminder of His Word and as a stirring of our hearts today back toward Him, our first love.

So there you have it—my confession. I am writing about something of which I have little knowledge, some experience, and a belief in what God asked me to do at this time. Interesting what God will ask of any of us at any time.

In my life, denominational experiences were limited but well lived out, so, readers, you will not find a condemning treatise about denominations in this book. It is very much my belief that God allowed the existence of denominations for a reason for a season; you will find no condemnation of any denomination. Being born to an Italian mother, lived in Italy for several years, how couldn't I become a Roman Catholic, even though I grew very weary of tuna fish every Friday. As a child, I had no choice. I believe my mom would have had a serious issue with a daughter that was not following her religion, especially living in the country where the Pope was residing. Heaven forbid! I aged; I found Jesus and became a Baptist and finally a non-denominational person. At this point, someone may be thinking, "Bless her heart (I do live in the deep South); she was just looking for Jesus and still is." I get it, but I would respond quickly that because I know Jesus, He trusted me to write a book about being a member of His church in unity with all others that call Jesus their Savior in hopes to be a part of the pure, unblemished bride of Christ called to the marriage supper of the Lamb. All that God instructed me to do was write His message about the divisiveness of denominationalism within His body of Christ. He certainly did not offer any instructions on what to do with this message; I believe He is leaving it up to you, the reader, as to what to do with message.

Any other denominational experiences or knowledge written into these pages will be from observations, discussions, and research. Denominations have been a part of my life, and for a long time, belonging to a denomination was the safety, security, and structure of a denominational church that held my attention, my attendance, and my allegiance. This book journeys through the changes from one denomi-

nation to another that led me to believe God gave me a revelation that denominationalism is not to be a part of His plan
for unity found in the unblemished bride of Christ.

CHAPTER 1

What Exactly Is Denominationalism?

In the world of Christianity, a denomination is a group of believers that follow an established doctrine, a predetermined set of rules or standards to which all in that group agree to follow the terms, conditions of membership as determined by the leadership of that denomination. No, this description is not meant to sound like a description of a country club nor a corporation. Churches do not focus on golf, pools, and dining rooms nor climbing the ladder to success; at least I am hoping this is not the case.

There is much more to the word *denomination*. While a denomination is a group grown out of a certain sect or belief, this is not to be confused with the word *denominationalism* which is an umbrella that illuminates, covers, and validates the concept of the existence of the number of denominations bringing emphasis to a need for separate, independent denominations. Further, denominationalism explains that, at some point in time, people decided that all the followers of a certain form of Christian beliefs needed to separate out from other fellow believers and build a denomination that fit their own very specific belief system or their personal interpretation of God's Word that became their theology. And then another group and another group followed suit and so on, and denominationalism opened its huge umbrella covering all denominations justifying the split of fellowship and the unity of the body of Christ! Thus, denominationalism spread as denominations became the fetch thing to do causing denominationalism's explosive spread throughout the world.

There are thirty-four Christian denominations worldwide (thecompletepilgrim.com, 2023). This number boggles my mind. How can there be so many differences in believing in and trusting the same God, the one and only God? What are the differences? What makes one denomination different from another? Still another question pops into my brain: Who sets up these differences? A larger question could be not just how but why do so many differences exist? Could it be that "these people come near to me with their mouth and honor me with their lips, but their hearts are far from me. Their worship of me is made up only of rules taught by men" (Isaiah 29:13). Keeping in mind I am not a theological scholar, my thought is the world of seminary trained theologians could provide a multitude of answers to all of these questions; however, still begging the question, Why have their answers not satisfied our human hearts? Why are current answers supporting separatism rather than unity among all believers? Oh, to write a book that provides all the life-giving answers so that all believers would experience the joy of being in fellowship and join hearts and hands and become that spotless bride! Well, come to think of it, that Book already sits on millions of people's coffee tables or bookcases; that's right. The Bible has already given us these answers if we would just believe the inspired Word of God with an inspired, genuine heart.

As I write these paragraphs, my spirit is still asking God these very questions! There are pastors, ministers, lay pastors, and believers all over offering their very best as devout Christians to bring unity to the body of Christ! My prayer is that God continues to bless these brothers and sisters with all the strength possible, and we know that a prayer offered in the will of God and believing this prayer will be answered; yes, that prayer will be answered! And that's worth a huge hallelujah and amen!

Here's a story about a couple of these inspired, devoted ministers. A short while ago, my husband I and watched the movie *Jesus Revolution*, based on and inspired by the life of Greg Laurie. Two other men helped Pastor Laurie onto God's path for his life: Chuck Smith and Lonnie Frisbee, Pastor Smith being an ultra-conservative pastor and Lonnie Frisbee being a hippie pastor ordained by his freedom to love Jesus without a seminary degree or kissing anyone's ring. At first, my husband and I, both being from the sixties era of rock and roll and free love (my husband is an old rocker; I never got into the rock and roll thing, and neither one of us believed in the free love action), we were both hesitant about what we were going to see in this movie. I can tell you the movie is inspiring! The truth that an entire generation of lost youth—under the powerful influence of the enemy's voice through ungodly music (now I confess, I did like The Monkees; they were all so cute!) and a free-flowing stream of drugs—seeking truth, God's truth, in good places and bad places was so well-portrayed in this movie that you were drawn into the struggle and the passion of this group of people as they were led to Jesus. Young, disillusioned about our country's government, corruption in the churches, and the destruction of the American family, prayer taken out of school, everything they were taught as kids just went out the window along with respect and dignity. Respect for any institutionalized religion and their own personal dignity was destroyed as they scratched out their existence sometimes in trash cans, the streets, and sometimes by the grace of God and local churches that saw that these kids were truly a lost generation. Yes, the sixties brought out a great deal of negativity and pain by a full-blown drugged society whose heroes died in some instances of suicide or overdosing. Yet somehow, some of those flower-wearing, tambourine-banging, pot-smoking band of lost souls stepped out of the darkness into the light because of people like Chuck Smith, Lonnie Frisbee, and Greg Laurie! Out of a genuine effort of seeking God's face and His heart, His freedom came to be the deliverance of their lives; they became Christians, in some cases much to the disdain of the suited men taking up the Sunday offerings and the beehive-haired women in the choir!

Reader, please know I mean no disrespect to any lady wearing a beehive hairstyle or a gentleman wearing a suit taking up the offering. It's just that, sometimes, people get so caught up in how people look, conservative and hippie, a suit-wearing gentleman and a druggie that has not bathed… which of these is God more concerned with? Which of these did God create his or her soul? Which of these does God love? The answer to all of these questions is He loves them all equally. But somehow, in churches today, not everyone is welcomed into the unity of fellowship, just like in the sixties. Churchgoers in 2023 are no different. I am just saying it is difficult to encourage and build unity with legalistic, man-made rules about appropriate and not appropriate dress is considered a priority to salvation and fellowship. I can almost hear the strains from a song about a company in the sixties "…not hiring long haired, freaky guys need not apply. So, I took off my cap and imagine that…" Now you know, my husband still indulges in some of his sixties' favorites; he tells me it's a history lesson!

Well, in my heart, today's youths are, unfortunately a throwback, a dangerous throwback of the sixties. I hear from so many teens today about their search for meaning, their search for God, the search for truth. They tell me they are confused, lost because one church says this or that about God, and the church down the road or around the corner says something opposite. I hear them repeat news broadcasts that this priest was held on charges of sodomy, molestation, and that pastor embezzled money from this church or ministry. Then the question comes, Why does God allow bad things to happen to good people? Some teens, youth, tell me that they don't know who to trust nor who to follow, so they just don't. Their thought is, *What's the point?* Youths went through a Goth movement and believed that to be their refuge; the darkness of the Goth movement thought this darkness was their solace. Sadly tragic for those that fell to this movement—a movement built on distrust, disillusionment, and lies. Many times, young people just don't trust anyone in any church; they don't follow any leadership in church, and so they just quit going to church.

The youth search for the same thing all of us adults seek: the truth. All of the haranguing, backdoor approaches, and well-intentioned lectures of us adults often end up driving the youth in the opposite direction. Youth tends to reflect some of the same attitudes that we adults put out! We adults are as apt to complain about the sermon of the day or gossip about what Miss Nellie wore to church. The old saying that children are like sponges is true; they watch, they listen, and they absorb!

Adults want to know God, and those that have a genuine heart for God reflect that love and a seeking heart for the truth of God; however, those that are just checking a box by attending church and doing all the Christian activities but in their hearts, the relationship with Jesus is lackluster, lukewarm. In Revelations 3:16, God lets us know how He feels about the Christian that just checks off the box: "So because you are lukewarm—neither hot nor cold—I am about to spit you out of my mouth." This was the word that God spoke over the church of Laodicea; we are not far away from this same church in our behaviors as Christians today.

What would it have looked like when Paul asked the group in Acts, "Have you received the Holy Spirit?" The group said they had not; they were baptized by John. Then Paul laid his hands on them, and they received the Holy Spirit and began speaking in tongues. Can you imagine what that must have been like for those folks having just received the greatest gift—the Holy Spirit! (Acts 19:6–7). If ever we need this passion, this power, it is now! What would a body of believers look like? What could be accomplished if a body of believers joined together with this passion and this power? I believe everyone that genuinely loves Jesus wants to obey God; He is seeking the parts of the body to come together and be the unblemished bride of Christ!

Feeling that you belong to some group is a strong, driving emotion for youth and adults alike. A lack of belonging can happen to youth, children in a traditional family as well as a blended family or a one-parent family because perhaps that family is just attending a church and not taking Jesus home with them. It happens to all of us in different seasons of our lives. Disruption of our day-to-day life due to all sorts of circumstances, probably too numerous to mention, and anyone reading this book probably knows these circumstances far better than I. What has this to do with denominationalism? Many times, people that seek that place of belongingness, never anchor in to any one church, any one denomination, because they have visited and visited and heard the varying perspectives of all the many places they have visited and accepted none. These folks never found relationship within any of the groups they visited for whatever reason. Some of these lost ones never attached or joined a church or a denomination because the feeling of belonging was never experienced at any of the locations they visited. Perhaps, this is how so many other denominations came into existence; just maybe some of these folks may have believed, they could do church better. So they decided to do church better and struck out on their own, in their own denomination, with their own church; thus, the independent church began to grow.

Answering questions about God and His Word can be a daunting endeavor, especially to children, youth. With so many different denominations vying for the attendance, allegiance, and loyalty of everyone and anyone, how does one make a choice? And, by the way, as adults, don't we find ourselves questioning the things of God? Why, yes, we do! Why then do we get so very out of sorts with teens and adolescents when they question? I believe that teens and adults question why churches operate the way they are and why God allows certain bad things to happen to good people. We are allowed to ask God these questions, and often, the answer can be found in His Word. Legitimate questions with answers that not all people, youth and adults, receive with an open heart can be discussed and researched; this is not a demonstration of a lack of faith but rather a lack of knowledge. Sometimes, God simply wants us to wait until heaven is our home to find some answers. I happen to be one that believes that not all our questions will be answered, anywhere. He simply wants us to trust in Him. In the grand scheme of life in God's kingdom, sometimes, these questions and thoughts become distractions from God's love for us and the gift of His Son, Jesus.

On the other hand, I have found it a good thing to question, to inquire about the things of God. David did that a great deal, and God said David was a man after His own heart (1 Samuel 13:14). God wants us to seek Him. He wants our full surrender to be to Him, and in order for us to do that, He definitely wants us to know to whom we are surrendering to. This is a journey at best, not a one-and-=done decision made when a child has experienced a delightful, fun-filled vacation Bible school or Sunday school class. Neither of these events are bad or wrong, not at all, but a child's mind, a child's spirit, and a child's heart is hungry for the purest of truths; God wants that child to be filled with the purest of truths: the Good News of the Gospel of Jesus Christ—undiluted nor manipulated nor tainted by man's interpretations that try to make a one-size-fits-all theological mandate that children are sometimes coerced into believing because that is what Grandmother believed and Mama, and therefore, the child must believe.

Let me clarify this a bit more. If as a child grows and he or she searches for God, and God leads him or her to that same belief system as Mama and Grandma, then perhaps that is the place that sweet child needs to be. But if as the child grows and genuinely searches for God and finds that

God is found in a different place then prayerfully, Mama and Grandma will serve that child well to hear him or her out about where he or she has found God. Just so you know, I really enjoyed my Sunday school classes and my catechism classes. I especially enjoyed the vacation Bible schools I attended, and no, I was neither hurt, damaged, or misled by any of the precious ladies that led me in these classes. However, as a child, I did what all children normally do: I simply believed the way I was told to believe no matter if it was a different belief from what I had learned from the year before from a completely different set of teachers from the same denomination.

My journey began when my mom took me to church and explained to me that this is where the family would always go, and there were steps I would have to attend in order to belong. Being the dutiful child, of course, I did everything I was instructed to do in order to belong. Pictures are in the album of my holy confirmation along with my brother's pictures in his suit for his Holy Communion—a big day for the family. Yes, it was a big day…me all dressed up in my little girl wedding gown and my brother in his black suit and tie. I had a veil and everything, you know the long white dress, white gloves, as did all the other girls. And so the day went; I really didn't understand all that was taking place. I just know I think the adults around me wanted me to understand, but full confession, I just plain didn't. Unfortunately, it took years for me to understand fully what I did not understand, and that was a bit nerve-racking for a young adult who had thought she knew mostly who she was and who God was in her life. What I did understand was I felt empty all those years, and worse, I felt so ashamed of myself for going to church and not admitting I didn't understand all that was going on. I felt lost; I felt alone, and honestly, I felt angry at myself. Sitting in church, going to youth activities, listening to the priest, and seeing my brothers and parents watching and listening did not fill that wondering and wandering in my heart. Years passed, about thirteen to be exact. My life was not in a good place; I was not attending any church.

I was twenty-three, working at a meat-processing plant. Lunch breaks found me reading a little book that opened my heart to more questions than I could ever answer on a lunch hour. The book was *The Nun of Monza* by Mario Mazzucchelli. The fact that it was about a nun named Virginia Marie (my birth name) might have influenced my decision to read this tragedy. However, what I took away from this book was a brokenhearted view of religious authorities. Oh no, not the nuns and priests; these were the authorities of my childhood. These were the people I trusted, believed every word they spoke whether I understood their words or not. This book shattered all that; I could barely put what I had read together enough to make any sense of it at all. Unfortunately, the book is based on a true story, and I felt I had stumbled across a big, ugly secret of someone's life. While the book messed with my heart and mind about religious authorities, I did take away from that book that people, many people, including religious authorities, leaders, may know about God, but they don't know God. They just go to church and come back home and live life just the way they always have and in the ways they wanted to live. This just didn't seem to be how I wanted or needed to be. After all, Scripture tells us in Haggai, "Now this is what the Lord Almighty says: 'Give careful thought to your ways" (Haggai 1:5 NIV). I had a lot of careful considering to do about my ways!

Looking back on that experience, I find myself so grateful. This was a door that led to my salvation. Because I couldn't fit into the current religious denomination, I told people I belonged to and had participated in; as a child, I began to look for where I was supposed to fit. "Afoot and lighthearted I take to the open road, Healthy, free, the world before me, The Long brown path before me leading wherever I choose" (Whitman,1856, Song of the Open Road). Whitman expressed exactly what I felt at this moment: I was on a journey, and I felt great about this adventure to find where and what God had for me. Being totally honest, even saying these words, "So I left the Catholic church" make me nervous. Leftover feelings from a person reared in a religion that leaned into the law, rules; mostly man-made rules lead me to nervousness any time I discuss that era of life.

What has all of this got to do with denominationalism? I realized that going from one denominational group to another and not knowing God was not necessarily the denomination's fault but my own. So I remind you, precious reader, that this book is not about slamming any denomination. However, experiencing multiple denominations throughout my life taught me that knowledge of and relationship with our Creator, our sweet Savior Jesus Christ, belongs to no denomination. A greater revelation was that knowledge of God and relationship with our Savior is two entirely different situations. Knowledge of God comes from hearing the Word, reading the Word, and living the Word through our personal relationship with Jesus, the Christ. This relationship belongs to the one who seeks and receives Jesus Christ as his or her Savior and Lord of his or her life. Further, you do not have to be a registered member of any one group to have this relationship.

Throughout my journey, I found that belonging to a church, to a denomination, allowed fellowship with other believers, but it was not my anchor to God. My relationship to God, my love of Christ is not under the umbrella of denominationalism; it is solidly forever abiding in Christ and Christ abiding in me. The church I attend allows fellowship with other like-minded believers that all experience the freedom of the Holy Spirit and the security of knowing how very much God loves them based on their knowledge and their relationship with God, not their membership in a church.

Denominationalism speaks to division rather than unity. One of my favorite books of the Bible is Joel. At this point, I feel a need to tell readers, again, that a theologian I am not! However, I do have some thoughts about Scriptures; I so appreciate grace being given to these thoughts! Back to Joel 1, the first chapter describes a decline in the strength of the church or a wandering away from God. Joel tells us, "Wake up, you drunkards, and weep! Wail, all you drinkers of wine; wail because of the new wine, for it has been snatched from your lips." The New Wine represents The Holy Spirit according to some commentaries, and this means that the churches are empty of the Holy Spirit. Considering the culture of today, Joel 1 could have been taking a picture of America today. "A nation has invaded my land, powerful and without number; it has the teeth of a lion the fangs of a lioness. It has laid waste my vines and ruined my fig trees. It has stripped of their bark and thrown it away, leaving their branches white" (Joel 1:6–7 NIV). One of the most powerful examples that comes to mind is all the varying religions that have rooted in America. These groups did not assimilate into a Christian America with a heart for unity in Christ—the foundation of this nation. Perhaps those early pioneers of this country felt that since religions other than Christianity were growing, maybe it was alright for individuals of Christian faith to set up and establish churches, denominations, that fit their personal perspectives, much like the differing religions that were permitted to grow in America.

> I am the true vine, and my Father is the gardener. He cuts off every branch in me that bears no fruit, while every branch that does bear fruit he prunes so that it will be even more fruitful. You are already clean because of the word I have spoken to you. Remain in me, as I also remain in you. No branch can bear fruit by itself; it must remain in the vine. Neither can you bear fruit unless you remain in me. I am the vine; you are the branches. If you remain in and I in you, you will bear much fruit; apart from me you can do nothing. (John 1:1–5)

We need fellowship; sadness comes when fellowship all together is just not happening, has not happened, and I am wondering how it is going to happen. I do know that while I am waiting for unity in the body of Christ, I have a job: being obedient to whatever God hands me to do—without question (please know I say this with great trepidation)!

God's Word emphasizes unity with Him. How can unity exist with Him if there are so many differing opinions on how we can have relationship with Him. We are "…like the branch…" that is His vine. How many people have a passionate desire to belong, to be a part of, to be wanted by a church family? Those numbers appear to be growing because the numbers of people leaving churches is growing—wandering believers that cannot find a pasture in which to feed. So many rules, so many differing approaches to the path of belonging has caused this exodus in addition to broken trust in church leaders that have stepped away from the faith or found to be fallen because of one temptation or another laid at their feet by the enemy. God wants to protect us by keeping us as His children, "I am the vine; you are the branches. If you remain in me and I in you, you will bear much fruit..." (John 15: 5).

Figs were first introduced in the garden of Eden when Adam and Eve had made their world-changing decision to snack on forbidden fruit. Genesis 3:7 tells us, "They sewed fig leaves together." Why? To cover their nakedness; they thought their sin was covered up, not so. Elsewhere in scripture, God uses fig trees as a sort of time clock: "Then He told them a parable: 'Behold the fig tree and all the trees; as soon as they put forth leaves, you see it and know for yourselves that summer is now near. So you also, when you see these things happening, recognize that the kingdom of God is near (Luke 21:29). Timing is critical to God's kingdom, and He said to watch the fig trees. Sin and timing—two concepts that God takes under strict consideration when His children are involved and engaged in His kingdom. He neither wants believers acting out of His time concerning His Will for their lives nor does He want His children in sin. However, these two concepts have divided so many groups of believers into the vast numbers of denominations. How?

Have you ever been in that conversation about the end times? Or that conversation about pre-trib, mid-trib, or post millennium? Interpretations and opinions based on

Scriptures vary so very much that division comes far easier than shared thoughts. God says in Matthew 24:36, "But about that day or hour no one knows, not even the angels in heaven, nor the Son, but only the Father." His Word appears, simply put, simple…no one knows the day or the hour. So why the arguments? Just how many branches are out there that belong to the One Vine? That explains that many branches can exist because of the multitude of reasonings, thoughts, and personal interpretations, but God's will is they must all be connected to the One Branch, not multiple trees and thousands upon thousands of varying branches. How did God design man? God designed man to have fellowship all together under one God, attached to one branch Himself. First Corinthians 12:12–13 says, "The body is a unit, though it is made up of many parts; and though all its parts are many, they form one body. So it is with Christ. For we were all baptized by one Spirit into one body…" establishes once and for all that it is appropriate and good that all over this globe, groups of believers are praising Him, but it has to be known that all these groups are branches from the One True Vine.

CHAPTER 2

What Does God Think about Division Among His Children?

God thinks much of unity—not so much of division, especially among His children! Traveling all the way back before Christians were called Christians, before the church in the book of Acts, before Antioch, Paul referred to believers as the ecclesia. Ecclesia means a gathering of believers called together by an authority. The etymology of the word comes from the Greek roots "ecc" meaning "assembly" and "kaleo" meaning "to be called out by a higher authority." People wonder from whence were people called out? A legitimate question for true believers with a very strong response. These believers were called out of the world to be in unity with one another and all together living with the same purpose, same goal, same priority. Another question, why would God call them out of the world? God wanted a group of people unified in the goal of establishing His kingdom on earth but not in the ways of the world. Key point being the people needed to be unified together striving to build His kingdom His way, and His way is that all are in Him, and He is in all that believe and accept His Son, Jesus Christ. This term has been around for quite awhile since 625 BC. Revelation 2:6 says a lot about a church that separated itself out; this is what Jesus says to the church in Ephesus: "But you have this in your favor; You hate the practices of the Nicolaitans, which I also hate." There exists a veil of obscurity covering the originations of the Nicolaitans, but a common thought is that Nicolas, one of the chosen seven deacons, fell off the path of God and became one of the renegade leaders of the Nicolaitans. Various authors have described the horrors of the Nicolaitans; God expressed great disdain for this group. This is one group that set itself aside; it was not "called out" nor a part of the ecclesia.

John 17:11 tells us, "I will remain in the world no longer, but they are still in the world, and I am coming to You, Holy Father, protect them by the power of Your Name—the Name You gave Me—so that they may be one as we are one." A bit later it says, "I in them and You in Me. May they be brought to complete unity to let the world know that You sent Me and have loved them even as you have loved Me." Jesus knew His time on this earth was up; He was headed home to His Father. It touches my heart to know that this precious Savior was more concerned with our well-being than what He was about to face. He wanted His Father to be in us and us in Him so that we could all be in unity in God's kingdom on earth and in heaven. So questions about God and His thoughts toward unity began when the people of this earth were being called to join together in assemblies that all became known as the ecclesia; unfortunately, some learned scholars consider Christianity's origins as a cult that moved into a sect as did many people in Paul's time: "However, I admit that I worship the God of our fathers as a follower of

The Way, which they call a sect"(Acts 24:14). More discussion about the cult thing a little later. Jesus's life demonstrates how God feels about unity and division.

Looking at Matthew 12:25, "But Jesus knew their thoughts and said to them: 'Every kingdom divided against itself is brought to desolation, and every city or house divided against itself will not stand.'" Most assuredly, many biblical scholars will offer not only varying opinions but also complete opposite opinions concerning the fact that God does not respect division among His church members, especially in the church age.

Considering the definition of the word *division*, "…to separate into parts or the process of separating into parts." Of course, division brings positive results in many situations of which you can use your imagination. Some of the situations of division that God approves were the parting of the Red Sea (Genesis 14:21–22) and separating out Korah's men from Moses's camp (Numbers 16:28–31). God's Word tells us in so many books of the Bible that separation is a necessary situation. In some instances, separation was to save lives; in other events, separation was part of a life vow as was the case of Samson (Judges 13:3–5). However, the key to our discussion is the separation of members of the kingdom of God.

A family member recently said, "One of the biggest disappointments in my life has been denominations (Mayer, 2022)." Why would this be a disappointment to anyone? Anyone can have an opinion about this statement, but what is the root of the disappointment? Was this family member hurt by a denomination? Actually, yes, he was. There was a time in his life that he wanted to be on the mission field and was very willing to go through rigorous training. However, the first step was to contact that denomination's board to check out the criteria to go out onto the harvest fields. As it turned out, his denomination would not allow a divorced person to go out onto the mission field because he would not be a good example of God's Word. This man was genuinely hurt, confused, and angry. He taught Sunday school and participated in his local church (he was a deacon). How did this happen? Why would he not be a good example of God? I know many folks who would have agreed with the denomination's decision. It definitely was the right of that denomination to set up its own standards and stick to them because that is how denominationalism works. However, several folks did express how sorry they were about the board's decision because it was wrong. I often wonder now, with the huge numbers of married missionaries coming off the fields, would he still be considered unworthy?

God's Word soundly reflects the importance of unity in the body of Christ. Throughout my years of wandering, my heart would bounce from one thought to another, especially as a child about being together in my Catholic Church while some of my friends went to a Baptist Church and some to a Methodist Church. Somehow, even at that age, I wanted us all to be together. Maybe, just maybe, in my child's world, I was missing my playtime with my friends, but as I grew into a youth, my thoughts went to wanting to be with my friends to be in "unity" with them about God, my holy Father. I wanted to do service works with them; I wanted them and myself to be learning about the same God and in the same way doing the same things. Strange as it was for a child and a youth, the concept of being all together under one roof with God was such a beautiful dream! Somewhere, someone planted a seed in my spirit, "So we, being many, are one body in Christ, and everyone members one of another" (Romans 12:5). Another seed came through these words:

> Far above all principality, and power, and might, and dominion, and every name that is named, not only in this work, but also in that which is to come: And hath put all things under his feet, and gave him to the head over all things to the church, which is His Body, the fulness of Him that filleth all in all. (Ephesians 21–23)

We, the body of Christ—the remnant, the believers in the life, death, and resurrection of Jesus—are the ones that make Jesus's life mission fulfilled. His Father gave Him all things (that would mean us as well) and everything else in this world. We are together in my heart, and we are supposed to be together in everything we do as a Christian family under the dominion and care of Jesus and the fatherhood of God.

Being all together as one church...sound familiar? Absolutely familiar! Of course! The church in the book of Acts has unity in action for sure—the perfect picture of unity actually.

> They devoted themselves to the apostles' teaching and to the fellowship, to the breaking of bread and to prayer. Everyone was filled with awe, and many wonders and miraculous signs were done by the apostles. All the believers were together and had everything in common.

Selling their possessions and goods, they gave to anyone as he had need. Every day they continued to meet together in the temple courts. They broke bread in their homes and ate together with glad and sincere hearts, praising God and enjoying the favor of all the people. And the Lord added to their number daily those who were being saved. (Acts 1:42–47)

This chapter is about what God must think of unity in His kingdom and the division of His children. The scriptures speak loudly in Acts 1:42–44 about what a church in unity looks like in God's kingdom. A couple of words from these scriptures really hit home when we consider joining with everyone else. Look at "devoted themselves to the apostles' teaching and to the fellowship, to the breaking of bread and to prayer." We have many, many in the kingdom that have devoted themselves to their denominational theology or to the church to they have attended but have not devoted themselves to those believers outside their denomination's kingdom. Sometimes, I get a vision of people running out to perform missional duties and run back to the safety and refuge of their denomination or church. Please keep in mind that I am not a theologian nor am I advocating for everyone in a church to rebel against their denomination. I am advocating that we might need to return to the structure and operational foundation of the church in the book of Acts. Here's a challenge question for you: how different would your church look from the church in the book of Acts? If you answered that there would be no difference, then I would challenge you to see how many folks in your church would sell all their belongings and give to those in need. What a tool of measurement that would be, don't you think? I think so!

Obviously, if a worldwide poll were taken to answer the aforementioned question, very few would genuinely say yes to the selling of homes and goods and distribute the money to the needy. Some would, and it stirs hope in my spirit that yes, there are some that would do this very thing. Mother Teresa comes to mind immediately! On this point, many of the churches could pass for twins of Mother Teresa. However, divisiveness exists on many levels and in just as many forms.

At this point, I think we need to look at the differing types of divisiveness existing in the body of Christ today to help develop a more accurate picture of how fragmented the body of Christ has become. I remind myself during this writing to keep focused on our Father, God, the Father of Jesus Christ. His Word is Holy Scripture, and the last words in Revelation 22:18–19 says,

> I warn everyone who hears the words of the prophecy of this book: If anyone adds anything to them, God will add to him the plagues described in this book. And if anyone takes words away from this book of prophecy, God will take away from him his share in the tree of life and in the holy city, which are described in this book.

In my journey, I remember times when reading His Word, my heart would question, my mind would wander into areas of interpretations, my interpretations. Sometimes, I would think or even speak out loud the scripture in my words; many people do that to gain some understanding or meaning to what God's message might be. I believe God is okay with that type of scrambling of His Words. However, if I were to have started sending out messages as to what His Word means with a definitive interpretation that strays from the truth of His message, then there would be genuine trouble for me because God said there would be trouble to anyone adding to or taking away from His Word. So divisiveness can occur when differing interpretations actually take away or add to His Word. Case in point, the issue of homosexuality. God's Word is clear on this topic: homosexuality is an abomination (Leviticus 18:22, 20:13; Romans 1:26–28). This book is not a debate about this topic; His Word is His Word.

While agape love is the fuel and backbone of the heart of a genuine Christian, and agape love is what we want to extend to those that have chosen the path of homosexuality, nowhere in God's holy Word does He instruct us to make the homosexual a better homosexual by agreeing with or condoning their behavior or teaching them how to better exist in this world as a good homosexual. Theologians of all sorts have written much about this topic with some saying that the scriptures need to be read in context with the times. Again, I say, His Word is clear on this topic historically and currently. Churches today are splitting based on this topic; this is divisiveness on a very high level. Case in point, the Methodist Church is going through this divisiveness experience right now. Other churches or denominations have been formed because of this topic; some churches being totally comprised of homosexual individuals have come into existence. As this is being written, a certain popular church leader has come under attack because of his viewpoint that homosexuals should be applauded because they "keep coming into churches where they know they are not accepted. They have more faith than I do" (Stanley, Andy, YouTube, 2023). This one topic has caused a great deal of the dissipation of unity within the body of Christ.

Beth Moore, one of the most talented, gifted Bible teachers chose to walk a path of believing that it is a normal part of some people's lives to be a homosexual and that Christians are being judgmental and homophobic by not embracing this lifestyle [support].

However, other types of behaviors, theologies contribute to the disunity of the body of Christ. Racism being a factor of dividing the body of Christ does not garner that much attention, but it should. Black churches, white churches, Oriental churches, Spanish churches, I get it. People want to be with their like-minded, skin colored, and culturally similar brothers and sisters.

Many of these aforementioned churches have purposely aligned with certain political parties, and their fundamental belief system moved away from God and more toward weaponizing their worship of God into worship of their communities and their communities alone. Unfortunately, some of these same churches have made it known clearly that they do not want to have any type of unity because unity would bring with it accountability to God and His kingdom.

Here's a short story, an example of how this has played out: I was invited to speak at a church in the community; it was an African American church. I got up and gave my little talk about Christian counseling and the value of this service especially in our little rural area. I felt that I had included everyone in my talk, and I felt that everyone heard the message. The next speaker got up, and I knew this speaker from another time in my life; I was comfortable with this young man because, to me, he was a precious gentleman. He started speaking, and the more he spoke, the more uncomfortable I grew. He started passionately decrying the bad treatment of African Americans and how they have to stand together because the white community was not their community. I kept thinking, *Hey! Do you not see me sitting right here not two feet away from you?* Obviously, I could not get up and leave; that would have been rude. I have to say, it was a struggle for me to keep myself from walking out vowing to not come back to that church. Bad attitude? Without a doubt! Wrong attitude? Without a doubt!

Here is where the lesson of forgiveness comes in. God spoke loudly and clearly: "How else do you expect unity and brotherly love to grow if you keep the divisiveness alive through unforgiveness?" I would really love to say I started a unity in the community group; I did not, but God did work on my heart, and I asked for His forgiveness! And the best thing, God forgave me, and that freed me up to desire complete unity with everyone! I learned I needed to pray for the speaker that had been so very offensive. I learned to pray for all communities different from mine! A side note, the pastor of that church, to this day, never realized nor recognized that a person sitting in his church had been wounded by the words of the speaker, and I pray his heart would have changed had he known this.

The heart of man is one of the key components to divisiveness. I don't know if the pastor from my little speaking experience knew what the speaker had planned to say, or if he felt confident, he wouldn't say anything that would wound a fellow human being. The point is his heart. This pastor did invite me, an older white woman, to come into his house of worship to speak. He had a heart for his parishioners to know about the information and message I carried to this community about the need for and the value of professional, cost-free Christian counseling. Whether I am white going into an African American church isn't the key; the key is the pastor was willing to unite two worlds. God created our hearts to love, and we are to love one another. We may not agree theologically; we may not agree academically, but above all, we need to agree to God's plan of one, unified body of Christ sharing in the bride of Christ as one.

So far, I have not seen in His Word that heaven will have these divisions for all our souls. Language barriers are obstacles that can be overcome. We can still worship God and be with God together even with seemingly unattainable resolutions to these obstacles. How this can happen takes a greater mind than mine; God knows how this can happen, and I feel that He has a plan. The thing is, I believe part of His plan was for us to start practicing being all together before His full plan takes place!

CHAPTER 3

The Unified Body of Christ

The terms Christians and divisiveness seem at odds with each other in principle, yet only minimal efforts appear across the globe to bring unity to the body of Christ. Please, readers, those of you whose church is trying desperately to join other churches in service and honor of God, you deserve all the blessings God can give. However, not all churches are making these efforts, and for the most part, the efforts are minimal; otherwise, would we not see growing efforts, massive efforts, toward bringing about the bride of Christ, the unified body of Christ? I think we would. There exist many unified groups across the globe, but not all groups are calling for the body of Christ to be in unity, not even all the Christians are working toward this unified body.

Any group that unifies brings a spirit that reflects the core beliefs of the organizers. Think for a moment of all the groups that have unified over the centuries; these groups were not without leadership. Leaders are powerful in the arena of influence and accepted power. A unified group will behave and perform according to the mindset, values, and goals of the headship of the group if loyalty is a core force in the membership. Think of how the Roman Empire spread or the Ming Dynasty or the Egyptian Empire grew; all these groups were unified under the leadership of some of the most powerful influencers of all time.

Ancient groups gave way to contemporary groups that unified under powerful leadership. Unfortunately, some of these groups don't exactly make it into the history books because of their sterling achievements. Groups like those led by Malcolm X, Jim Jones, or Hitler. Before joining oneself with a group, be very aware of their beliefs, their behaviors, and their goals. All unified groups set goals for the group; the extant problem is that not all goals are for the glory of God.

Unified groups generally offer many benefits on differing levels. For example, some feel safe belonging to a group that shares the same mindset or beliefs they do. Another benefit some garner from being a member of a unified group fulfills their deepest need to belong. Other group members passionately serve through the unified group to which they belong; this behavior allows these group members feel as if they have purpose in life.

In contrast to the precepts presented in the previous chapter concerning division, unification does not divide; it multiplies. Jesus had only two fish and three loaves; after praying and making the offering to His Father, the disciples had to pick up twelve baskets of leftovers; the tiny offering from the little boy was multiplied greatly because of God's blessing. When the disciples received the Holy Spirit, they went out into the world, and the numbers of Christians were exponentially multiplied!

God's creation included all the believers to live in peace and harmony with one another. Looking at our planet, knowing and seeing and being here with all the cultures of the world, it is almost impossible to understand how the body of believers can unite into the bride of Christ. God's Word tells us that in the last days, a remnant would be left:

> I ask, then, has God rejected his people? By no means! "For I myself am an Israelite, a descendant of Abraham, a member of the tribe of Benjamin. God has not rejected his people whom he foreknew. Do you not know what the Scripture says of Elijah, how he appeals to God against Israel? 'Lord, they have killed your prophets, they have demolished your altars, and I alone am left, and they seek my life.'" But what is God's reply to him? "I have kept for myself seven thousand men who have not bowed the knee to Baal." So at the present time there is a remnant chosen by grace. (Romans 11:1–5)

There are many other scriptures that speak to the "remnant"—a unified body of believers. Historically speaking, we know through Scripture that division came early on. Abraham's son Ishmael, born to Hagar, branched out to form a completely different nation than did Isaac. Division shows how other people feel their thoughts, their beliefs, stand up and over God's called-out people. Hundreds of groups organize, flourish, and may or may not succeed; keep in mind though that success is measured by God's standards, not man's.

CHAPTER 4

The Church or the Institution

This article, "The Misunderstood Reason Millions of Americans Stopped Going to Church: The defining problem driving people out is … just how American life works in the 21st century" (*The Atlantic*, August 2024) by Jake Meador opens with a startling picture of the church or rather the institution of church in America today.

> Nearly everyone I grew up with in my childhood church in Lincoln, Nebraska, is no longer Christian. That's not unusual. Forty million Americans have stopped attending church in the past 25 years. That's something like 12 percent of the population, and it represents the largest concentrated change in church attendance in American history. As a Christian, I feel this shift acutely. My wife and I wonder whether the institutions and communities that have helped

preserve us in our own faith will still exist for our four children, let alone whatever grandkids we might one day have.

This change is also bad news for America as a whole: Participation in a religious community generally correlates with better health outcomes and longer life, higher financial generosity, and more stable families—all of which are desperately needed in a nation with rising rates of loneliness, mental illness, and alcohol and drug dependency.

Have you visited a church and drove away thinking, *Wow! That was the sweetest church I have ever visited!* Then you visit again. You decide to join this church. Pretty soon, you begin to hear that the church needs money, and a fundraiser is coming up! You have been asked to please participate in this fundraising campaign, and they are going to train you on how to do this. There is just one little problem: you hate fundraising, and you hate asking people for money unless perhaps there are children involved. That could change everything; you are still uncomfortable asking for money, but for children, you would do it. The elders of the church, along with the pastoral staff, have decided that your new church needs a gym/fellowship hall. After all the research they read, they concluded that this building would draw new members to the church from the community. They have hired a consultant to lead them through this fundraising effort, and the first thing this consultant recommended was to get everyone on board, and that included you!

But you are new in this church, and maybe, it will make you look bad if you don't do this. Of course, there are many churches that would absolutely let you off the hook in this case and move on. You being you though decide to talk to the associate pastor about this most uncomfortable situation. He greets you, and after about twenty minutes, he tells you that it is your duty to help the church; in a furtive effort, you volunteer to count the money for the fundraiser or maybe you stuff envelopes. You offer all sorts of individual help, but he is adamant that going out door-to-door will help you grow as a Christian with no explanation as to how and why he felt you needed that growth. You had been in church all your life and dedicated your life to God.

Now, do I believe this happens to every church? Not at all! However, all churches have that person, that one person, that does make decisions about the growth of the congregants and their relationship with God without wisdom, just opinion, and outward observation. There are many in positions in the institutional church that use the power of their position that the institution has conferred upon them to mold the congregation into who they believe the congregation should be instead of allowing the Holy Spirit to do the molding of the participants into the people God created them to be in His kingdom. This is what the book of Ecclesiastes said, "There is nothing new under the sun." Governments and nations, fueled by the ruling religious powers of the day, have risen and fallen on the power, desires, and will of the leaders, the religious leaders. Check out the holy Roman Empire! The church was institutionalized a long time ago!

Once upon a time, in a very tiny town in rural America, a very dedicated Christian went to a deacon's meeting. His entire family had been so proud when he got elected; the deacon nomination was not a surprise; this was a beloved gentleman! This deacon loved helping people; his duties began as an usher and a Sunday school teacher to young boys. One of his favorite jobs was helping the senior citizens to their seats, and the little senior ladies just loved him for it! If these little ladies could have voted twice for the deacons, they would put in two votes each for this guy! I think it was his blue eyes, but that little band of senior ladies would have argued that point! After all, they were the ones with silver hair and a whole lot more wisdom than him at that point in my life! However, as time passed, this dedicated deacon began to feel strange about working for God in a church that felt more like a bank. His analogy became, "This reminds me of a bank; a bank helps people, but it makes sure they are making money while they do it." Such a sad analogy. The next deacon meeting fueled this gentleman's focus on the popular phrase, "What would Jesus do?"

So the meeting began, and he sat and listened as people made fun of local people, discussed their tax losses, and complained about their wives' spending habits, but when the fun stopped, they got down to business, and I do mean business. The business of the church became their business, and the church was being run as a business; money became the top topic. They took a deep dive into the goal for the night: being sure the church was solvent and making sure the tithes are coming in from the appropriate demographic group. This demographic group comprised of the twenty-five to forty-five age group was considered to be the moneymakers for the church.

I should say this group was considered to be the supporters of the church. This was not a new a topic of discussion; as a former Sunday school director, I was privy to the many staff discussions of how to be sure the church was taken care of monetarily. For the most part, I was in the dark because I was under the impression God would take care of the church; He said He would in His Word if we follow His standards for living. At any rate, I digress!

The more the discussion revolved around money and setting goals for a stronger reach out to the right demographic group that could support the church, this dedicated Christian grew uncomfortable. Finally, a saturation point was reached in his heart.

The dedicated deacon told one of the old-timers that a church should not be run like a business like the world runs things. He explained his belief that the church should regularly reach out to everyone to see about their needs, their joys in life, their sadness about loss, not just a visit to the money folks. We should not be running the church like a business.

The old-timer got highly offended and said, "Why wouldn't we do that? Most of us in this room are businessmen. That should affect how the church is run! That's how we are supposed to do things! That's how we get things done around here! How else are we supposed to make this church work? That's how we have always done it!"

The dedicated deacon asked, "Where is our trust in God in all this? Aren't we supposed to bring the light out to the world, not the darkness of the world into the church?"

Well, I will leave it up to your imagination as to how the rest of the evening went in that deacon's meeting. God spoke to me early one morning and clearly said, "The moment man seeks success through the guarantorship of man's institution for his church, the church becomes man's institution" (August, 2023). What exactly and when exactly did church begin? Did the church in the book of Acts go out seeking the moneymaking group? I don't think so.

Some say Christianity began as a cult then moved to a sect and then became an ecclesia. Any group, be it a cult, sect, or ecclesia exists because some level of organization exists. Remember Stephen? He was one of the seven chosen to help serve the Grecian widows after the Grecian Christians complained that they were being left out in the distribution of food by the leadership of the church in the book of Acts. This leadership group had been chosen by Jesus, and for two thousand years, this leadership style is the one that God expects us to follow. Understand that the distinguishing feature among what defines a cult, a sect, or Christianity lies in the leadership and the goals of this leadership. While cults and sects generally are led and inspired by the men and women who create them, Christianity, its first name being the ecclesia, was inspired by God, the Father, and the goal of Christianity was to worship and honor God, our Creator, Jesus, His Son, and the Holy Spirit. The other goals were to love one another and help all brothers and sisters in genuine need.

Christianity has been operating for centuries under the divine inspiration of God, not men. God, the Father, the Holy Spirit, speaks to man, and those that listen have been those that excel in establishing God's kingdom because it has been done by God. Has every church been impure in its ministry? No. We can never forget that Jesus knows the hearts of men, and they are not always pure in their hearts, even ministers, priests, and any of the number of workers under the name of Jesus. The good news is, Jesus came to save us, not condemn us. So please know that this section of the book is not a condemnation of denominational congregants or denominational ministers.

Let's remember John's last book: the book of Revelation. What about the seven churches of the book of Revelation: Ephesus, Smyrna, Pergamum, Thyatira, Sardis, Philadelphia, and Laodicea? God showed John the ills that had befallen each of these churches; there were only two that surfaced with a decent appearance to God: the church of Philadelphia and the church of Thyatira. God, the creator of all on earth, also records all on earth. Isn't it wonderful that we are not the ones that are to judge anyone or any church or any denomination? The responsibility on our shoulders is to be sure we are right with our Savior, individually, and do all we can to reflect His love onto everyone in unity as the bride of Christ. Are there churches that are perfect in this behavior? The behavior of reflecting God's love is the question. Without a doubt, I am sure there are churches that do reflect God's love in some way or even many ways, but the bigger question is, are they reflecting God's love in unity with all other believers? Is this a big ask? Certainly is! But is it too big for God? It is not; it is His desire that we all be together in heaven, and it is my thought that He wants us to be together in heart and mind on earth. God gave us a clear example of this big ask in the form of the church in the book of Acts.

It does take money to run a church. Okay, I have said it, so some that are reading cannot say, "This old girl doesn't know a thing; she is ignorant of the how to run a church!" They would be correct though; I have never run a church, but I do understand light bills must be paid, and staff must be paid and so on. Should the need for money stop any church from being like the church in the book of Acts? Some would say that the church became institutionalized by instituting the rules of the world's financial standards; that is to become a successful church measured by the world's standards to draw more people to their doors because they were financially well-off as evidenced by their savings accounts, the big family centers, or the road trips their members would take. This type of activity has led many a well-intentioned soul to become an idolater because money has become his or her idol; money has become the world's idol. Who believes that God's kingdom can be institutionalized? Not many would say that because it sounds awful! Unfortunately, for some churches, some denominations, money has become a driving force leaving behind God's mandate to love each other as He has loved us.

Sure, many have used the word *institution* when referring to religion. For example, I have heard many learned people say, "The institution of religion has…" and there are many differing options to end that sentence; I would think many of you could fill it in with the statements you have heard. Many of today's denominations have made an institution of their church to be their priority goal, and they have made their denomination their kingdom.

The institutionalization of the church is worldwide. Sadly, because of the various denominations, it is difficult to understand which institutional pattern the church is following. Churches are to follow Jesus's structure for the church. The issue is people believe he or she knows the structure based on his or her interpretation, and that is just not always the best pattern. The disciples tried this thinking a couple of times and were about as successful as I have been trying to think my own way through life. Remember the huge group of men, the five thousand? Yes, and the disciples wondered how this is going to happen and what to do: "As evening approached, the disciples came to him and said, 'This is a remote place, and it's already getting late. Send the crowds away, so they can go to the villages and buy themselves some food.'" Jesus had a better idea. Jesus always has a better idea. Institutionalization of the church demonstrates believers' attempt at making the church, God's church, better. No committee formed, no votes by a deacon board or board of elders, just five thousand well-fed believers experiencing God's miracle of life-giving sustenance through His Son Jesus.

People don't feel comfortable attending an institutional church. People are seeking a church that clearly and intentionally operates from the love of God and based on the premise that money is not to be the guiding goal of the church. I have sat in administrative meetings where this comment was made: "We must get more of the middle-class folks in. They are the moneymakers and will sustain this church." This is a true statement; it is a worldly built statement because it is based on trusting the financial basis for the church for its sustainability and its value rather than trusting God. I wonder how many times the church bookkeeper came to the deacons or elders and said that "the tithes and offerings are down. We are going to have to do better." Could some of these church members possibly sell some of their belongings or cash in a CD or take part of their savings and help the church pay their light bill for a few months or let the pastor and family come share meals with different church members? How original, right? Wrong! The church in the book of Acts did this, and what a church it was! God loved this church; He added members daily (Acts 1:1)!

Imagine for a few moments that your address is Dwelling Number 2, Antioch. Your home is one of the group of homes that have recently become believers in the life, death, and resurrection of Jesus Christ. It's time to gather your family to get ready to go the local meeting where believers are being taught how to grow in the Spirit and prepare the way for establishing God's kingdom here on earth. You didn't have to do anything to convince your family of the importance of this meeting time and the joy of being in fellowship with each other. How wonderful to experience the love of Jesus and how to love each other as genuine brothers and sisters in Christ. Your home, and the homes of many others, is the meeting place during the week to share this beautiful society in which each one looks after each other out of love and love only. There was no need for a welfare system; everyone helped each other if a need arose. Antioch was the first place believers were called Christians because these believers made the Son of God and the Holy Spirit and God the Father their life's priority.

This church in the book of Acts existed as God would have His church exist even today, taking care of the people, loving each other, sharing life with each other, under the leadership of those that know their calling is that of pastor, preacher, reverend, or priest. The goal of the church in the book of Acts was to go out and transform the world so that everyone could live having demonstrated Christlike attributes and successfully enjoyed God's peace, provision, and protection. There were no committees to bring forth growth in the church because everybody wanted to be a part of the church in the book of Acts and demonstrated that belongingness daily to the glory of God. To the church in the book of Acts, their church was not an institution; it was their spiritual anchor. The ecclesia was an assembly, a congregation; the believers of Antioch considered their lifestyle of living for Christ and honoring God to be the very definition of life. The power of Acts 1:8 explains that the power of the Holy Spirit was not for a select few that give more money than anyone else but that the Holy Spirit was for everyone, anyone, that accepted Jesus Christ as their Savior.

The church in the book of Acts represented the togetherness Jesus demonstrated while He was on earth, and the more I see of life today, the more that we can find no better model of Christian living than Jesus Himself. Think back to the third time Jesus revealed Himself to His disciples. He prepared a seashore breakfast for them of bread and fish (John 21:12)! Interesting detail, the book of Acts is all about unity through the brotherhood of Jesus Christ!

Remember in Revelation 2, seven churches were presented for varying reasons that God found important for not just the people of that day but for us today. Each church had either an issue or two that corrupted their body of believers or the church was doing something noteworthy to God's heart, just like the churches of today. Ephesus had walked away from their first love; Pergamum had folks in the church that were holding on to the teachings of Balaam and the Nicolaitans. God pointed out that the church of Thyatira had members that followed Jezebel! I believe one of His most difficult words was given to the church of Sardis; He reminded them they had a reputation of good deeds, and that they were alive, but He said, "You are dead" (Revelations 3:1). How hard was that to receive? Laodicea was a picture of many of the churches today; God said they were neither hot nor cold. They were lukewarm, and He was about to spit them out of His mouth (Revelations 3:16). The good news is that two of the churches were doing well in God's eyes: Smyrna and Philadelphia. Today, not all churches operate as if they are an institution, but many do. God is watching all our churches! Do you see any differences in that society and the society in which you live now? Yes, a multitude of differences exist;

chief of all, the personal love of Christ, the passionate love is very seldom seen in some churches today.

Worldly wisdom personifies entitlement. It urges us to find fault with ministries and assignments that we don't understand. Subtle boasting and pride are always at its root as it seeks to divide and weaken Christ's body. When we pattern our thinking about kingdom government after the pattern of worldly culture, two things can happen simultaneously: 1) we can actually give too much allegiance to one leader or ministry and 2) we can pull apart another leader or ministry when both are workers in His vineyard. The Corinthians were identifying with their leaders in unhealthy ways. Paul explained that they were acting as mere men (see 1 Corinthians 3:3) because their perspective of themselves and their leaders was based on worldly wisdom, which was holding them back from maturity. Instead of basing their identity on being new creations, they were viewing themselves and their leaders as "mere men." They actually found their identity in their leaders, comparing and exalting one above the other. Their identity had moved from being in Christ to being in certain leaders or ministries. "...For since there is jealousy and quarreling among you, are you not worldly? Are you not acting like mere humans? For when one says, 'I follow Paul,' and another, 'I follow Apollos,' are you not mere human beings?" (1 Corinthians 3:3–4) Here, Paul describes the comparing of ministries/leadership as a form of jealousy and quarreling. Jealousy can manifest by lifting one up and putting another down and quarreling over differences. Paul is appealing to the infant bride to stop comparing and to view themselves and their leaders through the lens of the Spirit. There is nothing wrong with human kings, but we are from another kingdom with one King. Of course, we still need national leaders, but this article is not about politics; it is about kingdom government established by God within His bride. The culture of the kingdom is not only formed by those called to lead but by the entire body of Christ. We are all responsible for the condition of the church in our generation. We are instructed to give our leaders double honor (see 1 Timothy 5:17) while still keeping God as the Lord of our lives.

True unity of the bride doesn't happen through unity gatherings or doctrinal agreement but through simply discerning Christ in fellow believers and respecting one another as coheirs. "By this everyone will know that you are My disciples, if you love one another." (John 13:35) A kingdom divided against itself cannot stand, and it is our season to stand, but we cannot stand without receiving our legs. We need them so that we can walk forward as the glorious field of God ready for the great harvest to come to us, for they are crying out for the sons of God to be revealed (see Romans 8:19). (Mandy Adendorff, Southington, Connecticut from The Elijah List, August 10, 2023)

This excerpt from Ms. Adendorff's writing in The Elijah List points to the reality that men can become so entrenched in the value, image, and traditions of their denomination or church that they give away their allegiance to the institution of the church instead of Jesus Christ. I have been just as guilty as any other church member in becoming so involved that my focus was on the activities of the church instead of what God was instructing me to do through the Holy Spirit.

CHAPTER 5

Point-by-Point and People Have Plenty of Points

We all have our own opinions concerning denominationalism. Remember that denominationalism is that umbrella that covers all the denominations in the world, and it grows exponentially. Many have said that there is no such thing as a genuine nondenominational church. Some have said their church is an interdenominational church. So many perspectives of God's houses of worship. Who is right? Who is wrong? This book opens the door to thoughts about God's kingdom, His perfect, unblemished bride: the body of Christ, the *unified* body of Christ. I believe a safe statement at this point in this book is that no one person or group has the answer as to who is right or wrong in the worship houses of God. Going back a bit, remember it was my hubby that asked me to think about why God would have me to write this book? This experience has taught me, more than ever, it's not going to be me or this book that unifies the body of Christ. So why, Lord? Why write a book about the unification of the body of

Christ? I believe this book to be a plow in the hands of those that read it. This book can till the ground for the planting of seeds for His kingdom. This book can be used as a harvest sickle in the hands of those that desire to be a part of the unified body of Christ—the unblemished bride. Seed by seed and one harvested field after another, we can be fruitful while we are waiting for the return of Jesus. We can each do our part to plant the seeds of salvation and/or start speaking to those that are saved to spread the good news.

However, those that defend denominationalism are strongly entrenched in the value of their denominations; they have strong deep roots in the growth of their denomination. They have strong historical foundations. The rise of denominations grew as the tapestry of the American landscape developed. From the pilgrims to the immigrants, both legal and illegal, culture and tradition came packed carefully in the knapsacks and their hearts. Once these folks hit our shores, those traditions and their cultural identity were the only things they had of normalcy in their lives. Some of their denominations survived to a degree but morphed into other groups. For example, the Amish were once a part of the Mennonite Anabaptists, but a schism in Switzerland caused a man named Jakob Ammann to become their leader, thus the name Amish. However, both Mennonite and Amish came to America and built their own kingdoms. However, some Amish and some Mennonites decided to leave the fold and began seeking other houses of worship. The following is an excerpt from a college's newsletter:

I'm a Mennonite for reasons that matter to me. But in the course of my conversations with Christians from other traditions, it has become more and more clear to me that all of history is ultimately moving to a time when all of God's people from every corner of the earth—all 38 denominations represented here at Goshen College, all 69 groups in our community, all of the world's 34,000 sub-groups of Christians, indeed, all of humanity itself—is going to gather together in praise to God. That's where history is moving. And I want to be on the side of history, finding myself on a path that is joining up with all sorts of other people who are also moving in that direction with the intention of praising the One who is seated on the Throne of God. If you are on that journey of bringing your praises to God, then hold your head high and sing out with gusto. If others are singing, then try to harmonize as best you can. (Roth, John D)

John D. Roth is a professor of history and director of the Mennonite Historical Library. This article is an abstract and distillation from his speech "Boundaries and Bridges: Do Denominations Matter?" which was delivered as part of the afternoon sabbatical series at Goshen College on February 12.

History is a precious thing. Many denominations take great pride in their foundations and will probably never walk away or allow their denomination to not be their safe place, their anchor, or their kingdom on earth. And again,

I say, neither myself or this writing will cause them to drop the denominational covering and simply be who we were called first at Antioch: Christian. Truly, Pastor Watchman Nee's story about the Holy Spirit being inside every genuine Christian soundly walks out God's Word; however, while we are united by the Holy Spirit indwelling in each of us, it is what we allow the Holy Spirit to do and how we consider our ways as we live and breathe with regards to our relationship with God, the Father, Jesus, His Son, and the Holy Spirit. Is the Trinity our priority or our denomination? This is the individual's decision, but it concerns the corporate, unified body of Christ.

The Roman Catholic Church, as it has since time immemorial, played a powerful hand in the growth of America's institutions that once were honored, revered, in America. The Roman Catholic Church helped the institution of education by building schools from primary to post-secondary (i.e., Notre Dame). Further, the Catholic Church influenced the political players that helped to grow America (i.e., the Kennedy Dynasty described so well in Taylor Caldwell's novel, *The Balance Wheel*). As time passed, other denominations migrated to America and built communities around their faith and cultural denominational traditions (i.e., Amish, Mennonite). Americans began looking at developing their identity which includes developing their own houses of worship built on their own theological foundations and their own denominations; thus, the umbrella of denominationalism grew.

Looking at America's houses of worship, one can see the great Catholic cathedrals built in the ancient images of their European heritages and the old country churches built of hand sawn lumber harvested from the nearby forests.

These are the houses of worship that hold the congregants of the multitudes of believers from all the differing denominations. Some singing or chanting from old Latin missiles to old songbooks published from the early days of America's birth. Today, many of those old cathedrals still stand; some of the old hand-hewn country churches have been carefully preserved—and how beautiful are all of these structures. In the same way, the theology of each has continued into current times—still separate, set apart from each other—as far as those cathedrals are from those old-time country churches. All worshiping the same God apart and by themselves.

One benefit considered critical in belonging to a denomination is the financial situations of churches, especially in the current temperament of our culture. Belonging to a denomination, in some cases, means those that belong to that denomination could be receiving funding from their cover or from the leadership that oversees the churches' operations. Some say this is a great form of accountability. However, along with the accountability comes strings attached to how the church is run, the theology that is offered by that church, and the rules and protocols of that church must fit into the box of the covering of that denomination. Just a thought, accountability to God needs to be the priority. God is the provider.

CHAPTER 6

Why Now and What to Do?

In conclusion, I wanted to continue the transparency and let you, the reader, know that even as I was headed to the end of this journey, I still had questions. For example, the question came to my mind as I meandered through these pages; why now, God? It's been several years since You first told me to write, and my excuses kept coming on stronger than my obedience! Yes, through the years of avoiding His command, guilt would sometimes wash over me, and I would feel there has to be a better word than awful, but at this moment, awful is what comes to mind! I did not deny Jesus, but I did turn away from His command; I won't compare myself to Peter, but he surely came to my mind several times for his behavior! Troubled, anxious, concerned…my heart and my spirit could not settle over this situation, and in my life, it was a situation especially when I tell others, "Listen carefully, and when He speaks and tells you something to do—not matter how foolish—just do it!" It is just as true for me as anyone else that runs, turns a deaf ear to God and His plan that your life is not exactly smooth sailing until you stop, turn around, and listen and obey!

In my heart, I knew I could not turn away this time; deep in that part of our being where our spirit lives, I felt not my urgency of what the times ahead hold for us Christian brothers and sisters, but His urgency about the times that we are facing soon and soon. Every Christian reaches that place of seeking God's will and His plan for his or her life. This book became a part of His plan for my life, and I realized that the urgency was real, and it was time to remind my brothers and sisters in Christ that we are to be the unified body of Christ, the bride of Christ. Fully realizing this writing is meant to be a reminder of who created us and for the reason of His taking the time to create us. I don't know and no one else knows the "the time or day" when Jesus returns. What I do know is I need to be aware, awake, and ready.

We all need someone to challenge us from time to time. For me, that would be my precious husband. As I began working on this book, he read, he edited for content and readability. One evening, he stopped me and said, "What are you going to say if someone asks you what your goal was in writing this book?" I thought, *He knows perfectly well what the reason for the book is*! He did know the original command from God to write the book, but he was wise to ask the question. After all, God gave the command to write about the impact of denominations on the church, His church, but why?

I believe that God is wanting us to seek a solution to the divisiveness of denominationalizing so that unity will reign in His kingdom. I believe God wants all His children to be in the body of Christ that will become the bride of Christ. The goal of this book is to stir thinking to encourage believers to begin the work of coming together and realize it will take work—the hard work of the heart and spirit. The goal of this book is to start the journey one page at a time. Speaking of time, how many of us believe that time is growing shorter and shorter before God sends His Son Jesus to gather His bride?

An amazing pastor/preacher/teacher and author, Watchman Nee wrote in his book, *The Normal Christian Life* (Tyndale House Publishers, Wheaton, Illinois [1980]):

> I was once with a group of Chinese believers who found it very hard to understand how the Body could be one when they were all separate individuals who made it up. One Sunday I was about to break the bread at the Lord's table, and I asked them to look very carefully at the loaf before I broke it. Then, after it had been distributed and eaten, I pointed out that thought it was inside all of them it was still one loaf—not many. The body was divided, but Christ is not divided even in the sense in which that loaf was. He is still one Spirit in us, and we are all one in Him.

Now, this is a very powerful picture that Pastor Nee presented, but what a wonderful picture of unity. Different cultures, different heritages, different skin color all together because the Holy Spirit indwells all of us; the same Holy Spirit unifies us all. Genuine unity of those who have the Holy Spirit in them demonstrates love, pure and wholly, for all our brothers and sisters in the same way Christ did. In the act of walking in Christ's command, the Bible says, "A new command I give you: Love one another. As I have loved you, so you must love one another. By this everyone will know you are *my* disciples, if you love one another." This is God's plan—His ultimate plan to have His church as the unified body of Christ. Further, Pastor Nee goes on to say,

> Yes, the Cross must do its work here, reminding me that in Christ I have died to that old life independence which I inherited from Adam, and that in resurrection I have become not just an individual believer in Christ but a member of His Body. There is a vast difference between the two. When I see this, I shall at once have done with independence and shall seek fellowship. The life of Christ in me will gravitate to the Life of Christ in others. I can no longer take an individual line. Jealousy will go. Competition will go. Private work will go. My interests, my ambitions, my preferences, all will go. It will no longer matter which of them does the work. All that will matter will be that the Body grows. (Nee, 1980, p. 219)

Take a close look at Pastor Nee's words, "My interests, my ambitions, my preferences, all will go." I find a curious thought in his use of the word *my* in this sentence. Denominations exist because it was all about the "my" of people that felt their way was the best way. However, in each denomination, hope exists because of the indwelling of the Holy Spirit in those that have allowed the "my" to leave their lives no matter what denomination they follow. Watchman Nee never promoted denominationalism nor divisiveness. The entire world recognizes diversity in cultures and people. God created diversity but for the divisiveness found in the kingdom on earth and definitely not in heaven.

A long while back, the Lord showed me an acronym that, to me, to my heart and spirit, meant a great deal. The acronym was SELF: *Satan's energy living through our flesh.* The door that the enemy often uses is our flesh, our self. Jesus went so far to say, "If anyone desires to come after Me, let him deny himself, and take up his cross and follow Me. For whoever desires to save his life will lose it, but whoever loses his life for My sake will find it" (Matthew 16:24–26). There isn't any room in the body of Christ for "my" being a part of any conversation concerning being a member of the body of Christ. The enemy will feed off hurt, wronged, damaged flesh, making it very hard for the person to lay down self and not use the word *my* in every general conversation that pops up. I think everyone of us have known that person that never spoke to anyone unless it was about his/her problems every time you came into his/her circle.

When the "my" or "self" becomes the guiding star to any one of us, we separate ourselves away from the body of Christ, thus bringing about more division in the body of Christ. Jesus's words in Matthew 16:24–26 suggest strongly that if we lose our lives to Jesus, we will find our lives in the body of Christ—the unified body of Christ.

After over two thousand years, divisiveness permeated all denominations; this destroys unity. God's desire is for all to come to the supper with the Bridegroom. God wants an unblemished bride—a complete and unified body of Believers. Revelation 19:7 speaks to the marriage of the Lamb and the bride, the Lamb being Jesus and the bride being the church. The concept of unity among all of God's children appears to be a critical part of God's heart. It behooves us to dig in and find the commonalities upon which all Christians can stand. Loving builds relationship; loving each other and those that need to know God as their Savior and know His Son Jesus and understand that the Holy Spirit is alive and well in us!

The ultimate goal of this book is to offer some constructive advice, yes, some "how-to" thoughts about bridge building among all denominations so strongly and with so many bridges that we become one in unity in the love of Jesus Christ and of each other. Watchman Nee's analogy of how one loaf of bread broken into bits and consumed by fellow Christians represents our unification by the indwelling of the Holy Spirit inspires such hope for the body of Christ, the unified body of Christ here on earth. Since we are not a loaf of bread, how can we, as brothers and sisters in Christ, do what Watchman Nee's loaf of bread did?

Remember the challenge to build bridges? Lots and lots of bridges? Three concepts are given below to show how these bridges are built:

1. *Teaching children the basics of the Gospel.* Start while the children are young. Jesus Christ is our Savior; He lived, died, and was resurrected for the bridge He built for us to get back to God and to eternity in heaven with our heavenly Father and Jesus together as the bride of Christ in unity. Allow children to learn in environments that promote unity

and not divisiveness. Celebrate unity in the body of Christ! This is a strong foundation for this bridge. Teach children to seek out ways to join with other denominations in worshiping God and honoring God together as the body of Christ.

2. *Nurturing, upholding each other in needs, honoring each other in service to each other.* As the body of Christ, we follow the church in the book of Acts in helping and loving each other in brotherly love. Join other churches together by having services together, church fellowships together. Seek to offer help to people with needs that attend other churches. Make it a priority to invite people from other churches to your events. When you help one of the "least of these," you have touched the heart of God because you are loving one of His children—another powerful foundational bridge back to God's unified body.

3. *Demonstrating lifestyle, daily prayer, reading and studying His Word daily, walking in His Word for yourself and all others of God's children.* This bridge is an individual effort that can involve sharing what you know with others, but it first begins with your commitment to building this bridge back to unity in the body of Christ. Commit to planting God's Word firmly in your heart, your spirit, by studying it every day. Arrange life events that include God as the focus and unity of the body of Christ as the outcome of the event. Praying for others as well as yourself, seeking out those that have needs in prayer, and acting on the needs while building the bridge of unity back to God.

Teaching, nurturing, and demonstrating were all of Jesus's ways of loving God's children without separation of theological premises developed by man, without division created by man's interpretation of God's Word. Just love, a pure love of the individual souls in unity, bound together by His pure love; Jesus went about teaching, nurturing, and demonstrating this love to everyone that allowed Him to love them. These three bridges truly lead to unity in the body! So many of you reading this are far more creative, far more along the path of unity than myself; use that creativity to increase the bridges that others need to be walking on to get back to the body of Christ!

Two powerful scriptures lay the foundation for one church, God's church:

> I have other sheep that are not of this sheep pen. I must bring them also. They too will listen to My Voice, and there shall be one flock and one shepherd. (John 10:16)

> You do not realize that it is better for you that one man die for the people than that the whole nation perish? He did not say this on his own, but as high priest that year he prophesied that Jesus would die for the Jewish nation, and not only for that nation but also for the scattered children of God, to bring them together and make them one. (John 11:50–52)

These two scriptures clearly demonstrate God's desire for there to exist the bride of Christ, full unity in the body of Christ.

Demonstration of living life as a fellow believer in a society striving for unity manifests in a plethora of spirit-filled, faith-filled activities. Think back to Jesus walking along the beach at the Sea of Tiberias as morning was showing itself. Simon Peter, Thomas, Nathanael and two other disciples were floating in a boat bemoaning the fact that after an all-nighter, they had no fish to show for their hard work. Coming to their rescue, someone that appeared to be a stranger on the shoreline shouted to them, "Friends, haven't you any fish?" To which the disciples respond, "No!" Then the stranger instructs them, "Throw your net on the right side of the boat and you will find some." Well, the haul was huge, and the disciples were shocked. "Then the disciple whom Jesus loved said to Peter, 'It is the Lord'" (John 21:5–6)! Surprises all around! Jesus had appeared, and this was after His crucifixion.

I genuinely feel that I probably would have done the same thing the disciples did after Jesus's death on the cross: I would have gone back to work! Up to this point, the disciples just felt that they needed to go to their homes and resume their everyday lives. But as the song goes, "Then came the morning…" Yes, then came the morning after Jesus's crucifixion, was anything different? Oh yes! Everything was different, but the biggest difference was the heart of man because something changed!

The disciples decided to trust this man on the shore and do something different; they cast their net on the other side. Think for a moment: how successful are our churches of today? Statistics abound pointing to a dire reality that youth are walking out of church and not walking back into the church. The youth are not the only population that are sitting out life ignoring the fellowship of believers. Unity does not abound in the church. Are we doing the same thing over and over just to find that what we are doing just isn't working? Could it be time for us "to cast our net on the other side?" (John 21:5). What do we need to do differently in our prayer life?

1. First and foremost, pray; seek God's specific guidance for what and how He wants you to work toward building those bridges unifying the body of Christ. Not everyone will have the same assignment or task because God is going to want everyone to utilize their gifts in this effort, and not everyone has the same gift. You might be the one that has the gift of hospitality; this would allow you to open your home to varying brothers and sisters in differing denominations for Bible study about God and His desires for all of us.

2. Prayer is always our first, best effort. Pray for denominational leaders to have the desire to come together as brothers and sisters under the covering of God and God alone. Pray for the boldness and courage to bring people back to God's Word about division in His children. If the neighbors or community ask questions, bring them back to Acts and how Paul defended his actions before the Sanhedrin, Felix, and the Romans. Remind them Paul had one goal: gathering souls for God's kingdom and the people's eternal home with Jesus—all under one God.

3. Pray for all the brothers and sisters to turn their eyes and hearts to God together in one body, the bride of Christ.

Not being a scholar, a professional writer, or an expert in any field, this book reflects an act of obedience on my part to God's command to write a book about how denominationalism has brought about divisiveness among His most precious creation: us, His children. Throughout the process of composing this book, in the back of my mind, I was hearing the voices of those that are scholars, professional writers, experts in the fields of biblical studies, pastors, and leaders of denominations expressing their great displeasure in the message of this book. Those voices have been turned over to God because, honestly, I could not move forward in my assignment with those voices speaking so loudly. So I asked God to please either plug my ears or get rid of the voices; He told me to get to work and focus. Reality dictates that voices will speak out for and against this writing, but I have been obedient, and my prayer is that no offense is taken because no offense was intentionally meant.

Moses knew he was standing on holy ground; Moses experienced the genuine fire of being in the holy presence of God. Further, Moses knew he was being tasked by God, not man. Abraham, in obedience, took his son up the mountain and was going to offer to God, in honor of God, his own son—the type and shadow of God's gift of His Son for our freedom. Point being obedience to God is priority. I am grateful that God told me to write this book; I wasn't a bit happy about this in the beginning, which we have already discussed, but I did come to my senses and got the book started.

Consider God's words to the angel of the church of Ephesus:

> I know your deeds your hard work and your perseverance. I know that you cannot tolerate wicked men, that you have tested those who claim to be apostles but are not have found them false. You have persevered and have endured hardships for my Name and have not grown weary. Yet I hold this against you; You have forsaken your first love. Remember the height from which you have fallen! Repent and do the things you did at first. If you do not repent, I will come to you and remove your lampstand from its place…He who has an ear, let him hear what the Spirit says to the churches. To him who overcomes, I will give the right to eat from the tree of life, which is in the paradise of God. (Revelation 2:2–7)

Has the body of Christ, the unified body of Christ, lost its first love? Is that why we have such divisiveness? Have our "selves" become more important than His body of Christ? What do we do to change and have Ecclesiastes exudes insight into truths about life? Before anyone jumps into a chasm of despair about our inability to know the answers to how and what we need to change to get back to God's design for us, consider some of these truths from Ecclesiastes. The state of churches today is not a new thing; denominationalism did not catch God by surprise.

What has been will be again, what
has been done will be done again; there is
nothing new under the sun. (Ecclesiastes
1:9)

Denominationalism is comfortable; denominationalism represents division of the body of Christ. I cannot imagine how God's heart has felt for all these years watching His
children scatter into all the different denominations that
appear to have taken His children's attention away from our
First Love.

The answer to the why question is, time is short and
getting shorter day by day. The urgency has set my heart,
my spirit, on fire to spread the word; come join the body of
Christ! Hurry, come be a part of the bride of Christ so you
can be at the wedding super of the Lamb!

What is the solution to the divisiveness? Radical, extravagant love. Love for our First Love: Jesus, and the demonstration of radical, extravagant love for His children. This
type of love prevents division and encourages unity, builds
unity and protects the body of Christ! Some, probably many,
will say, "That's easier said than done!" I get it! First of all,
what is extravagant love? What is radical love? For a person
that for the first time he or she actually reaches out to someone they have never even spoken to and says, "Hi! How are
you doing today?" That person would declare that was radical love for that person. On another note, another person
might give a huge donation to help feed a single mom and
her four children after the loss of her husband; for the first
time, this donor gave any money. This donor might consider
that extravagant love. While both acts of kindness are radical
and extravagant for each of the participants, when compared

to the residents of the church in the book of Acts, these acts of random kindness were a way of life, not a one-time won and done act. It's a heart change and soul-focused lifestyle of loving God's people.

In my humble opinion, taking baby steps and showing love to those around you that you have declared to be one of the "unlovables." You know who these folks are; these are those folks that have distinctive characteristics that goes against your grain. These are not the people that blow up towns and nations. Those would be termed terrorists! The unlovables are those like your Aunt Sara that you will make every excuse in the world to not show up to your mom's house for supper when Aunt Sara comes to visit. Why? She always wants to grill you as to why you believe the way you believe, why you drive what you drive, how much you are making now, and it just goes on and on! No, I would rather not break bread with Aunt Sara either, but what would God have us do? God would want us to sit down and ask Aunt Sara to pass the mashed potatoes with a smile! This is a life change: this radical, extravagant love for others, and it is possible. This would be a step toward building the body of Christ, increasing the unity God desires for His unblemished bride.

*****

Back at the beach…Daddy hugged his precious daughter tightly as he called to his little boy to come join their mama by his side. Mama wiped the tears away from her tiny daughter's eyes while Daddy whispered to his two bundles of energy. Mama listened intently to precious words of comfort offered to the owner of the destroyed sandcastle. He explained in the tenderest tones he could muster to his toddler that he was sure that God hated to see His sweet little girl hurting so badly. The little bundle of tiny sobs was watching and listening to her daddy's heart and especially to his discussion of God's great love for her. Her daddy went on to explain that sometimes we get busy doing things our way so quickly that we forget that Daddy reminded you about the waves. But Daddy loves you, sweetheart, and so does God. Sometimes, Daddy even forgets to listen to God, and I do things my way, and things don't go so well. But God still loves me too! So Daddy went on to explain to his little ones that some changes have to be made in order to rebuild the sandcastle, and if they would listen to Daddy, all will work out well. Without missing a beat, that sweet little girl looked up with the biggest grin and with the brightest baby blue eyes and told her daddy, "God always has the bestest plans, right, Daddy?"

"Why, yes, He does my little angel! Let's go build us a big sandcastle all together!"

Writing this book meant a great deal to Virginia Mayer; she felt that she had been obedient to an assignment given to her by God to remind people of His great desire for us to live in unity and make some big steps toward becoming that unblemished bride of Christ!

She wanted to honor God with her obedience even though, as she explains in the book, her obedience was not immediate, and it came with great trepidation!

Virginia loves her Savior, her family, and the work God has given her to accomplish. She and her husband are partners in ministry as the cofounders of Living Waters Counseling Inc. and Kingdom College—a newly founded institution of higher learning based on God's infallible Word.

Life is busy for Virginia, but never so busy as to not stop and give God the glory for all He is doing in this time and place!